The
Needlecraft
▬ Magazine ▬

BOOK OF

NEEDLEPOINT
STITCHES

A STEP-BY-STEP
STITCHING GUIDE

REBECCA BRADSHAW

future
BOOKS

This book is dedicated to my mother,
Sandra Bradshaw, who taught me to stitch
and continues to inspire my work.

First Published in 1994 by
Future Books
A division of Future Publishing Limited
30 Monmouth Street, Bath, BA1 2BW

Designed by Paula Mabe
Illustrations by Patricia Cuss
Edited by Juliet Bracken
Photography by Rob Scott

A catalogue record of this book is available from The British Library

ISBN: 1 85981 000 4

Printed and bound in the UK by Butler and Tanner

We take great care to ensure that what we print is accurate, but
we cannot accept liability for any mistakes or misprints.

—Contents—

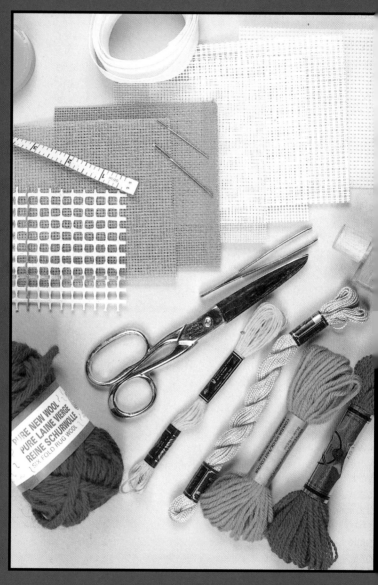

The Needlecraft Book of Needlepoint Stitches

CANVAS

Canvas is made in different ways and sold in varying mesh sizes. It is referred to in holes per inch or HPI. The finer the canvas, the more holes it has to the inch. Some canvas sizes refer to the number of threads per inch.

When choosing which HPI canvas to buy consider the type of design you want to stitch and what it will be used for. If the design has little detail buy a canvas with a lower HPI such as 10HPI or 14HPI. If the design has a lot of detail a finer canvas like 18HPI or 22HPI should be bought to ensure you have the space to add more detail. Remember that some canvases are more suitable for working without a frame.

Canvas is sold in different colours, most commonly white. Cream, brown and yellow, or "antique", canvases are also available. Choose the one closest to your thread colours. Some canvases with more holes to the inch are made in pastel shades. They are useful in pictorial work for when areas of the canvas will be visible, such as for the sky.

The price of canvas varies according to its quality. It is most commonly made of cotton, however, cheaper, synthetic blended canvas threads are also available. Always buy the best canvas you can afford as you want your finished work to last a long time. Look out for canvases which have threads of irregular thickness as this will show in your stitching.

When you have chosen the type and count of canvas buy enough to leave at least 2 inches (5cm) around the stitched area for blocking, framing and mounting.

The different types of canvases are:

SINGLE OR "MONO" CANVAS

This is formed by the inter-section of a vertical thread with a horizontal one. It is easily distorted if used without a frame but as it "gives" more it is useful for items like seat covers or footstools which curve.

It is not very good for half cross stitch as the stitches can disappear behind the threads. It is best for Continental Tent or Basketweave Stitch.

SINGLE/MONO INTERLOCK CANVAS

This is made up of two thin vertical threads twisted together and then twisted around each single thicker horizontal thread to produce a locked mesh. The process is completed by horizontal and vertical threads of the same thickness. It is more stable than single canvas but as the threads are thin they can shift and are difficult to stretch back into place.

DOUBLE OR "PENELOPE" CANVAS

This is formed by the intersection of pairs of vertical threads with pairs of horizontal threads. It is sometimes labelled with two numbers, for example 10/20. This means that there are 10 pairs of threads to the inch but 20 holes. It is stronger than single canvas and makes it possible for the length of the stitch to be varied. The stitches can be worked over two threads, one pair, as usual but on areas of fine detail like a face, you can stitch between the pairs of threads and double the number of stitches possible.

Double canvas can also be trammed. This process involves working long stitches across the canvas and then covering them with stitches in the same colour (see page 59). It makes the stitching more hard wearing and also means that you only need to follow the chart for the tramming stage. Some canvases are sold individually or in kits ready trammed.

RUG CANVAS

This is made up of two vertical threads which are twisted together and two horizontal threads twisted together. The vertical and horizontal threads are then twisted together at the intersection. The threads cannot be separated like double canvas. This strong canvas is mainly used for rugs.

PLASTIC CANVAS

This is moulded rather than woven into threads. It can be bought in sheets or ready cut pieces. It does not distort and is ideal for three-dimensional items like boxes as the canvas is cut to size first and stitched after. It can be sewn together at right angles. It is ideal for children or beginners and is easy to work with.

The Needlecraft Book of Needlepoint Stitches

WASTE CANVAS

This is made from canvas threads held together with starch. It can be tacked on to any non-evenweave fabric, such as clothing, and the design stitched through the canvas holes. The canvas threads are then moistened to remove the starch and removed with tweezers.

PRINTED CANVAS

This can be bought in individual pieces or as part of a kit. The design is printed on the canvas in colour and worked in threads of the same colour. There is no chart to follow which some stitchers prefer.

DE LUXE CANVAS

The threads in this canvas have been polished to give a better appearance. Although quite expensive it is worth the money as the thread slips easily through the canvas. All the stitches in this book were stitched on de luxe canvas.

THREADS

There are a variety of threads available for needlepoint which come in different weights, qualities, fibres, textures and colours. When choosing your thread you should consider not only the design you are stitching but also the type of canvas you will be working on.

The thread should be thin enough to slide through the holes of the canvas without distorting it, but also thick enough to cover the canvas beneath the stitches. Threads differ in thickness and weight depending on their "ply" and "strands". A strand is a unit of the thread and a ply is part of a strand.

Threads are sold with different numbers of strands depending on their type. These strands also have different numbers of plies. You can vary the thickness of thread used by separating the strands. The plies in strands do not separate very easily and it is not really recommended to do so.

Different types of fibres are used in needlepoint thread such as wool, cotton, silk, rayon and metallic threads. Wool is the most common one as it is quite strong and hard-wearing. Select a thread depending on how much wear your piece of stitching will get. For example, wool should be

Materials

used for a rug, but rayon or metallic threads for a picture.

The fibres in needlepoint threads are longer making the thread stronger so it is not advisable to use a knitting wool or other type of thread as a substitute.

The different types of thread are:

TAPESTRY WOOL

This is also known as *Tapisserie Wool*. It is a four-ply, single strand wool which actually works out finer than three strands of Persian Wool. The plies are difficult to separate so it is only really recommended for medium count canvases like 10HPI.

PERSIAN WOOL

This is a two-ply, three-strand wool, ie. each length of thread consists of three strands twisted together with two plies in each strand. The strands can be used singly or together according on the desired thickness.

Persian wool is a versatile thread as its thickness or "weight" can be adapted. Also, different coloured strands can be combined in the needle to create a variegated effect and give a wider choice of colours.

CREWEL WOOL

This is a two-ply, single strand thread which is most often used in crewel embroidery or, by combining a few strands, in needlepoint. It is a very versatile wool as colour combinations can be made by mixing the colours of the strands in the needle.

RUG WOOL

This is a thick, single strand thread used primarily for rug making. It is made in wool, acrylic and a rayon/cotton blend. The thickness varies with the fibre content and the number of plies.

STRANDED COTTON

This is a six-strand thread which can easily be separated to create varying thicknesses. It is most commonly used in cross stitch and embroidery but several strands can be used together in needlepoint.

COTTON PERLE

This two-ply, single strand thread is made in three different thicknesses: 3 –

heavy, 5 – medium, 8 – fine. It is a cotton thread and has a slight sheen. No. 5 is roughly the same thickness as Crewel Wool and gives a shiny contrast to a wool background.

Soft Cotton

This is a five-ply, single strand thread. It is soft to work with and has a matt finish. It is useful for varying the texture in needlepoint and is often used for Satin Stitch.

Metallic Thread

This is available in various weights, textures and colours. It is not hard wearing and should therefore only be used in small areas.

Needles

Tapestry needles are ideal for needlepoint as they have large eyes and blunt points. The eye has to be large so that they can be threaded easily and the blunt point stops the needle piercing and separating the canvas threads as you stitch.

Tapestry needles are available in sizes 13–26, size 13 being the largest. The finer the needle, the smaller its eye. They are also available gold-plated. These needles slip through the canvas better and are ideal for anyone who is allergic to metal. Tapestry needles can be bought in packets of mixed sizes or in packets of the same size. Change the needle for a new one when the surface starts to come off and the needle goes black. You will find it much easier to slip the needle through the canvas holes if you do this.

To decide on the size of needle to stitch with, drop it diagonally into one of the canvas holes. If it is the correct size it should rest in the hole and not fall through. And when you pull it through the hole it should not distort the canvas threads around it.

Frames

Mounting your canvas on a frame while stitching helps to keep the canvas neat and the tension of the stitches even. It also reduces the distortion of the canvas which is a common problem.

However, the most important thing to bear in mind is that you must work in the way you find most comfortable. Working with a frame does have its advantages but it is not very portable, especially if you stitch while travelling.

Many stitchers prefer to work with the canvas in their hand, then reshape it once complete. The only thing to remember is you should not switch from working without a frame to using one after you have begun stitching. This will alter the tension and it will be noticeable. Your canvas should not be wider than your frame but it can be longer so take care over buying a frame for your needlepoint.

There are several types of frame to choose from:

SLATE FRAME

This frame has top and bottom rods attached to side arms and kept in position by wooden or metal screws. These can be adjusted for several sizes of canvas. The sides of the canvas are laced to the side arms.

ROTATING FRAME

They are available in different sizes. The top and bottom roller bars are attached to side pieces and the canvas tightened with nuts. The canvas is stitched to the rods which can be rolled up and down as you work different areas of the canvas.

STRETCHER FRAMES

These are made from two pairs of wooden "stretcher" slats which slot together. The canvas is pinned to these slats. The frame should be just larger than the area to be stitched. The disadvantage of this frame is that it is not adjustable and can only be used for the one canvas size.

TUBULAR FRAMES

These frames are made from PVC tubes which are joined at the corners. The canvas is attached with half tubes which clip over it and on to the frame. The canvas is quick and easy to attach but it can slip so keep checking the tension and tightening the canvas if needed by rotating the half tubes outwards.

HOOPS

These are not recommended for needlepoint but are useful if you are only working small pieces of canvas. You can stitch the canvas around the outer edge to a piece of fabric then cut away the fabric behind it. Mount the fabric into the hoop and you can then stitch on to the canvas.

OTHER EQUIPMENT

There are various other pieces of equipment you may find useful when working needlepoint. Some are needed for stitching, others for stretching your finished work into shape, others for creating your own designs.

SCISSORS

Large dressmaking scissors are useful for cutting the canvas to size before you stitch. They need to be strong as some canvas is quite stiff.

Small embroidery scissors with sharp points are useful for cutting threads or snipping out mistakes.

TWEEZERS

If you make mistakes in your work you should snip the stitches and remove them with tweezers. This will prevent you from disturbing the other correct stitches.

TAPE MEASURE

A flexible one is best for measuring your canvas before cutting and also for counting the number of holes to the inch if your canvas is not labelled.

MASKING TAPE

This is used for binding the raw edges of the canvas before you stitch to prevent the wool from catching on the edges and snagging and the canvas from unravelling.

PINS

Large headed pins are used to attach the stitched canvas to a board when you are stretching it back into shape.

BLOCKING BOARD

You will need a piece of soft wood which is large enough for you to pin your stitched canvas on to when you are stretching it back into shape.

PERMANENT PEN

If you need to transfer a design on to your canvas it is best to use a pen. Take care not to use anything too dark for transferring or it may show through your stitching.

Techniques

The Needlecraft Book of Needlepoint Stitches

PREPARING

Once you have chosen your canvas, threads and design you can prepare to stitch. Cut the canvas along the threads into a square or rectangle remembering to add at least 2in (5cm) all round the outside of the finished design area. You should always work on a regular shaped piece of canvas whatever the shape of the design.

Bind the raw edges of the canvas with masking tape, to prevent the thread from snagging on the edges and the canvas from unravelling. If it is a large project or one that will be worked on for several months, stitch fabric tape around the edges, as the masking tape will eventually come unstuck. It is also better to use fabric tape if you are going to be working with a slate or rotating frame.

Fold the canvas lightly in half each way to find the centre and mark with a pencil. This is usually the best place to begin stitching.

Count the threads of the canvas out from the centre to find the outer edge of the design and mark the outline with a pencil or waterproof pen. This outline will be used later if you need to stretch your canvas back into shape when you have finished stitching. Place the canvas on a piece of thick paper like blotting paper, and transfer the outline of the design on to this. The paper will be used as a stretching template once the project is complete. You will find this step invaluable later, especially if the finished design is an irregular shape like a seat cover.

TRANSFERRING THE DESIGN

This process only applies to uncharted designs and should be carried out before your canvas is put in a frame.

If you are copying an image or drawing, draw lines down and across the centre of the drawing and do the same on the canvas. Matching these lines, pin the canvas over the picture. Using only waterproof paints or colouring pens, paint the design on to the canvas following the picture beneath and matching the colours as closely as possible. It is important to wait for the paint to dry before you begin stitching over it. Take care not to use too much paint or it may clog the holes. Always test the paint on a spare piece of canvas first to make sure that it is the right consistency and won't run.

Another way of doing this, instead of painting the whole area, is to draw only the outlines of the individual elements on to the canvas. This only applies to fairly large areas with few details.

If you have trouble seeing the details through the canvas you could tape the drawing and the canvas to a window so that the light shines through and makes the image a lot clearer.

PUTTING THE CANVAS IN A FRAME

Label the top and bottom of the canvas before you put it in the frame, so that you know which direction you are stitching in. With some designs this is not always clear until a fair amount of the design has been worked. This may save a lot of unpicking later on.

Once you have marked the canvas and made a template you can put it in a frame if you are using one.

Sew the bound edges of the canvas centrally to the tapes at the top and bottom of the frame. Use any strong thread for this. Attach the side arms to the frame; on a slate frame you will need to adjust the side arms to the required length then oversew the sides of the canvas to them. This is not necessary on a rotating frame.

On a stretcher frame, pin or staple the canvas to all four sides. Pin from the centre outwards on each side so that the tension is correct and the corners of the canvas are square.

STITCHING

You should not work with a piece of thread longer than 18–20in (46–50cm) as the constant rubbing of the canvas threads against it will cause it to fray and wear.

If you have difficulty threading the needle try a needle threader. Or, try folding the end of the thread tightly over the eye of the needle then slide if off while holding the thread tightly folded. You can push the eye of the needle on to this then pull the fold through.

To begin stitching, hold about 2in (5cm) of thread behind the canvas in the direction you are going to work and your first few stitches will secure this thread. Cut any loose thread ends so that they do not get pulled through to the front when you work further rows.

Another way to start is to tie a knot in the end of the thread and push the needle into the canvas about 2in (5cm) from where you will begin and along the line of stitching. Pull the thread tight and your first few stitches will secure the end of the thread on the back of the work. Cut the knot before you reach it.

To finish off the thread, weave it through the back of a few stitches already worked then cut it off close to the canvas. Try to avoid starting and finishing a thread in the same place as ridges may be noticeable on the front from the extra thickness at the back.

There are diagrams, photographs and instructions on how to work all the stitches in this book so all the information you need can be found later. However, a few general hints may be helpful.

The majority of the stitches should be worked using the stabbing method. This is when the needle is pushed through to the back of the work in one motion and out to the front in another. The other way is called the sewing method when the needle is pushed in and out of the canvas in one motion. The stabbing method is obviously more time consuming but you will find it creates a much neater and more even tension. When working in a frame you will find it easier to work this way as the canvas is held taut.

Some stitches require you to turn the canvas at the end of each row. Simply turn the canvas upside down and work the next row in the same way as the first. The stitches will still look the same, this is just an easier method of working.

As you stitch you will probably find that the thread becomes twisted and the stitches look uneven. When this starts to happen, stop stitching and hold the canvas so that the needle and thread hang down and untwist. Then carry on working.

When you come to the end of a stitching session, try not to end in the middle of a row as this will loosen the tension of the stitches already worked. Instead, finish off the thread before you stop. You should also move the needle along the thread to a different position now and again to prevent it wearing thin.

Wherever possible, bring the needle up into an empty hole and down into a worked hole. This can prevent the sewn threads from splitting. Stitching into a worked hole helps to keep the piece smoother by pushing the fibres downwards.

Avoid pulling the thread too tightly as you stitch. You can easily tell if you are doing this from looking at the canvas threads. If they have begun to move and no longer form straight lines, you are stitching too tightly. At the same time, avoid working too loosely or the stitches will sag and look uneven and will snag later, especially if your work is going to be a cushion cover or a footstool.

Practise stitches first on a spare piece of canvas if you are unsure how they are worked. You will usually find that your second attempt is better than your first.

If you are left-handed you may have trouble following the stitches in this book as they are all explained for right-handed people. However, if you turn your canvas and the book upside down you will find that you can follow the stitches much more easily and you will achieve the same result as a right-handed person. Follow the numbers on the stitches in the same order as shown.

WORKING FROM CHARTS

Some needlepoint designs are shown in chart form. You can work from almost any cross stitch chart. Choose one without any three-quarter or quarter stitches. Each square on this type of chart represents one stitch over one thread of the canvas – usually a diagonal stitch. Follow the symbols and the key for the correct position of your stitches. It is important to count carefully and often to save unpicking. You may want to colour in the stitches already worked on the chart.

Some charts have the stitches drawn in over the lines of the graph paper. This is very useful when different types of stitches are used. They are easy to follow but you must count regularly to check you are stitching correctly. It is easier to stitch correctly by working the main design first and the background stitches after.

Another type of chart is one on which an area is simply outlined and details of the stitch and the colour to work that area in are given in the key. Careful counting makes this easy to follow.

You can alter the size of your finished stitching when working from a chart simply by changing the size of the canvas used. The larger you want your stitching to be, the fewer holes to the inch your canvas should have. Take care when buying the canvas that you calculate exactly how much you need. For example, if a chart is 30x40 squares and you want to stitch on 10HPI canvas, you should calculate 30÷10 and 40÷10. This means that your finished stitching will be 3x4in (7.5x10cm) so, adding a 2in (5cm) allowance all round, you will need to buy a piece of canvas measuring 7x8in (18x20cm).

STRETCHING AND BLOCKING YOUR STITCHED CANVAS

When you have finished stitching lay the template you made at the beginning over the design to check if the canvas has distorted. It is quite usual for it to distort even when using a frame although obviously less so.

If there is little or no distortion you will only have to steam press it on the back to even out the stitch surface. Pull it gently back into shape and leave to dry thoroughly.

If the canvas cannot be pulled back into shape in this way, place your template on a piece of soft wooden board. Moisten the canvas on the back by spraying with water, then place it right side up on to the board and pin all the way round matching the edges of the stitching with the template. You may need to pull it very tightly in some places to make it square. Use a set square to check the corners of the canvas are at right angles.

—Diagonal Stitches—

Continental Tent

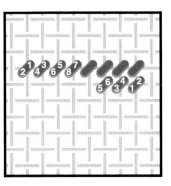

Working Instructions

Continental Tent Stitch is one of the most popular needlepoint stitches. It covers the canvas well and is especially useful for areas involving frequent changes of colour. This strong and hard wearing stitch is particularly good for rugs and footstools.

Always work back on yourself – if working from right to left across the canvas you should actually stitch from left to right. Follow the numbers on the diagram carefully before you begin stitching. At the end of each row you may find it easier to turn the canvas round to work the row beneath in the same way. The back of your work will consist of neat diagonal stitches.

Bring the needle out at 1, back and in at 2, out at 3, and so on. Follow the numbers on the diagram to work the next row whether or not you decide to turn the canvas round.

Diagonal Stitches

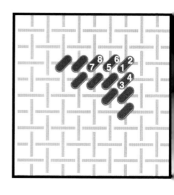

Working Instructions

Basketweave Stitch looks exactly the same on the front as Continental Tent Stitch except that it is stitched in a different way. It is good for covering large background areas especially where there are few colour changes and causes minimum distortion to the canvas.

This stitch consists of diagonal stitches worked over one thread of the canvas from one corner. Make several stitches up and then several across each time as on the diagram. Bring the needle out at 1, in at 2, out at 3, in at 4, and so on.

Working Instructions

Half Cross Stitch has the same appearance on the front as
Continental Tent Stitch and Basketweave Stitch but, again, is
worked in a different way. It is not particularly hard wearing.
Half Cross Stitch does not distort the canvas as much as
Continental Tent Stitch and is more economical on thread.

The back of the work is formed of rows of vertical stitches.
Bring the needle out at 1, in at 2, and so on. At the end of the
row turn the canvas round and work the row beneath. If you
find that the back of your work is formed of alternate vertical
and diagonal rows then you have been working Half Cross
Stitch and Continental Tent Stitch. This is a common mistake
to make but turning your work round at the end of each row
should help you to stitch correctly.

—— The Needlecraft Book of Needlepoint Stitches ——

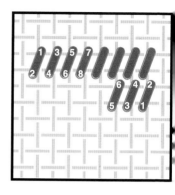

Diagonal Stitches

Working Instructions

Slanted Gobelin is worked in much the same way as Continental Tent Stitch and, again, is very hard wearing. It creates a striped effect which is useful for detail on houses. The stitches can be of any height but should not be too long or they will look untidy. You can adapt the height of the stitch to suit the area you are filling.

Bring the needle out at 1, in at 2, out at 3, in at 4, and so on. Follow the numbers on the diagram to stitch the next row, remembering to work back on yourself. You may find it easier to turn the canvas round.

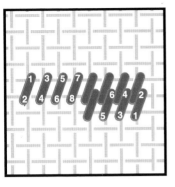

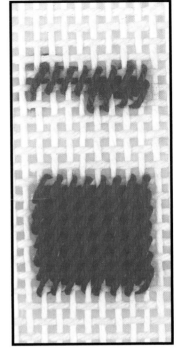

Working Instructions

Encroaching Slanted Gobelin is a hard wearing stitch formed in the same way as Slanted Gobelin. However, the rows of stitches overlap to give a more even, uniform texture. Again, it can be of any height to suit the area you are filling.

Work the first row in the same way as Slanted Gobelin, bringing the needle out at 1 and back in at 2, out at 3 and in at 4, and so on. Position the tops of the stitches in the next row one hole above the base of the stitches in the first row creating an overlapping effect. Stitch all rows in the same way making sure that the positioning is correct and that you form a diagonal stitch on the back of your work.

Scotch

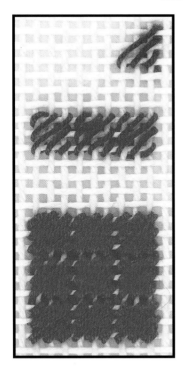

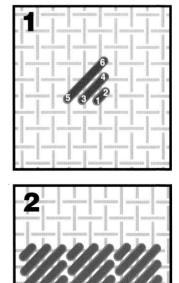

Working Instructions

Scotch Stitch forms a pattern of five diagonal stitches across the canvas. It is a hard-wearing stitch that is particularly useful for stitching walls and roofs, or creating a stone or tiled effect.

Bring the needle out at 1, in at 2, out at 3, and so on. Five of these stitches form one repeat. Work the next one to the left of it, stitching into the same holes as the previous repeat.

Condensed Scotch

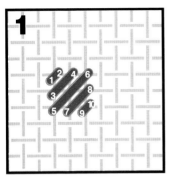

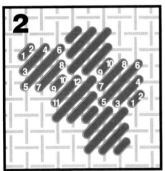

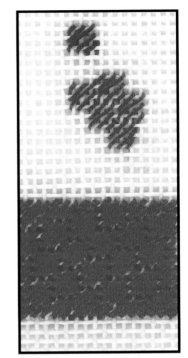

Working Instructions

Condensed Scotch Stitch is also known as Diagonal Ground as it is worked diagonally to cover the canvas. You can either stitch all rows in the same colour or, to add subtle shading to an area, gradually change the colour you are working with in each diagonal row. For striking patterns use two very different colours to make bold diagonal stripes.

Work one repeat in the same way as Scotch Stitch, then work the next one diagonally below this using the last stitch of the first repeat as the first stitch of the next one. In the next row, line up the longest stitch in a repeat with the shortest stitch of a repeat in the previous row.

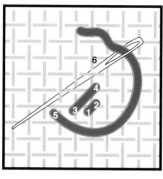

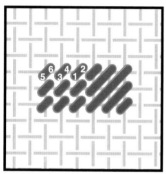

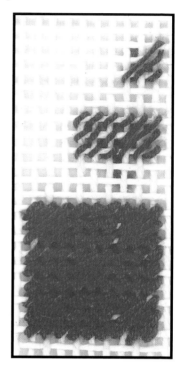

Working Instructions

Chequer Stitch is a variation of Scotch Stitch. It gives a good texture on the canvas and is useful for any area requiring a three-dimensional effect. Chequer Stitch is made up of alternate blocks of Scotch and Continental Tent Stitch.

Work one repeat of Scotch Stitch by bringing the needle out at 1, in at 2, out at 3, in at 4, and so on. When you have completed the first repeat, work another one of the same size next to it in Continental Tent Stitch, bringing the needle out at 1, in at 2, and so on.

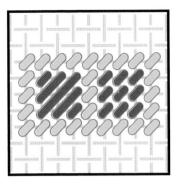

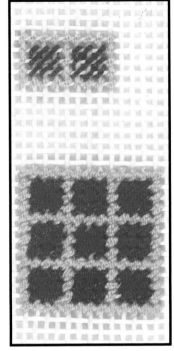

Working Instructions

Scottish Stitch is a combination of Chequer Stitch and Continental Tent Stitch. It is useful for filling large areas of the canvas and gives an unusual checked effect. Scottish Stitch can be worked in one colour but is more effective if the Continental Tent Stitch grid is in a different colour. You could also work the Chequer and Continental Tent Stitch repeats in different colours or work all the repeats in Satin Stitch.

Work the diagonal Satin Stitch repeats first over the canvas. Then work a same size Continental Tent Stitch repeat one hole away from each one – alternately beside and below it. When you have completed the desired number of repeats work the Continental Tent Stitch grid around them.

Cashmere

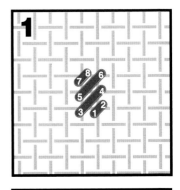

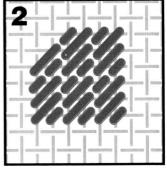

Working Instructions

Cashmere Stitch forms a rectangular block-like pattern on the canvas. It is particularly good for filling background areas as it gives texture and interest to the work. Cashmere Stitch can be worked in one colour or in alternately coloured repeats for a more interesting effect.

Work one repeat at a time by bringing the needle out at 1, in at 2, out at 3, in at 4, out at 5 in at 6, out at 7 and in at 8. Work the next repeat immediately to the left of this one. When you have completed the row in this way you will probably find it easier to turn the canvas upside down to work the next one.

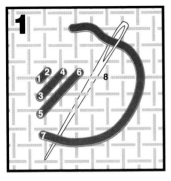

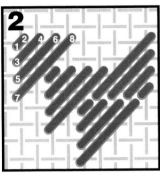

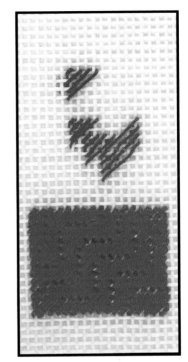

Working Instructions

Milanese Stitch creates a striking pattern on the canvas. It can be used to fill background areas but is most effective on abstract patterns, especially when worked alongside other needlepoint stitch patterns. As some of the stitches are quite long and the pattern quite big, it should only be used on large areas of the canvas and is best worked in only one colour.

Begin at the top left. Bring the needle out at 1, in at 2, out at 3, in at 4, out at 5, in at 6, out at 7 and in at 8. These four stitches form one repeat. Work the next one with the first short stitch in the centre of the row below the longest stitch of the last repeat. Continue in this way to the end of the row then stitch an adjacent row of repeats upside down lining up the shortest stitches with the longest ones in the previous row.

The Needlecraft Book of Needlepoint Stitches

Diagonal Stitches

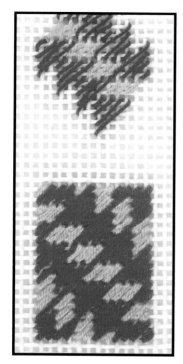

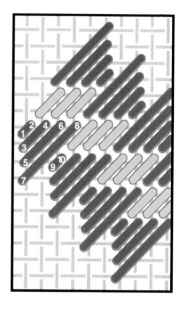

Working Instructions

Oriental Stitch is a variation of Milanese Stitch. Like Milanese Stitch, this stitch forms a large pattern and should not be used on small areas as the unusual stepped effect of the pattern will not show up as well. It can be worked in one colour but is most effective in two different colours.

Work a diagonal row of Milanese Stitches. Reverse the direction of the triangular blocks in the next row positioning the longest stitch of the repeats in each row diagonally next to each other. After you have filled the required area of the canvas in this way rectangular areas will remain unstitched. Fill each one with three stitches in a different colour.

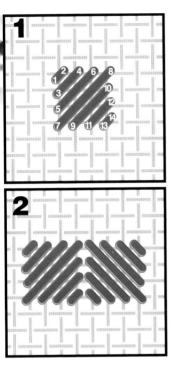

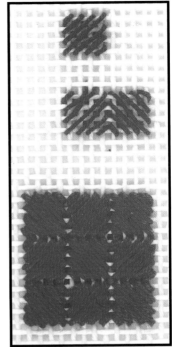

Working Instructions

Cushion Stitch creates a padded raised effect which gives an interesting texture to the canvas. It is useful for abstract designs or geometric patterns such as on a cushion cover. Cushion Stitch looks best on large areas as the greater the area worked the better the effect.

Starting in the top left-hand corner, bring the needle out at 1, in at 2, out at 3, in at 4, out at 5, in at 6, and so on. This forms one repeat. Make the next one touch the first one but reverse the direction of the stitches. When stitching rows of Cushion Stitch remember to alternate the direction of the stitches in each repeat.

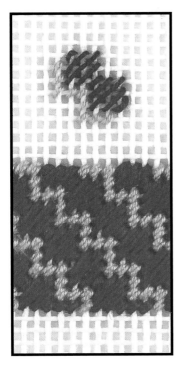

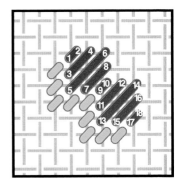

Working Instructions

Moorish Stitch makes a very attractive pattern that has a woven, zig-zag effect. It can be worked in only one colour but is more dramatic if worked in two as shown in the example.

Work the Satin Stitches first. Begin in the top left-hand corner. Bring the needle out at 1, in at 2, out at 3, in at 4, and so on, following the diagram. Work the next row one hole away. When you have covered the area, fill in the gaps with stepped rows of small diagonal stitches.

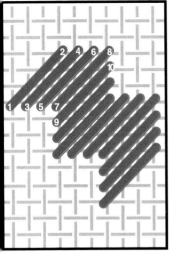

Working Instructions

Byzantine Stitch produces stepped rows of stitches and is an ideal background stitch. It is best worked over a large area of canvas as this makes the pattern more striking. It is usually worked in one colour but, for a more striking effect, work each row in different colours. The stitches can be made over any number of threads but they should all be of the same length. Do not make the stitches too long or they will look untidy.

Bring the needle out at 1, in at 2, out at 3, in at 4, and so on. It is important to count the number of stitches in a row before changing direction as it is easy to make a mistake and then the adjacent rows will not line up together. Once you have completed one row, work the one above in the same holes as the previous row.

 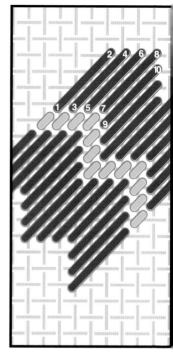

Working Instructions

Jacquard Stitch is worked in the same way as Byzantine Stitch except that a one-hole gap is left between each row. It works well on large areas of the canvas, as a background stitch or on abstract designs. Work the small diagonal filling stitches in a different colour to create a stepped pattern.

Work all the rows of diagonal stitches first, following the diagram and leaving one hole between each row. Fill in the spaces with small diagonal stitches in another colour.

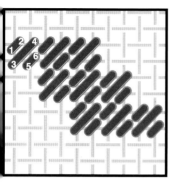

Working Instructions

Mosaic Stitch forms a small closely woven pattern which is
ideal for backgrounds requiring a dense pattern or in smaller
areas. It has a very neat appearance and can be stitched in
one colour or in alternating blocks of colour for a bolder effect.

Begin in the top left-hand corner with a small diagonal
stitch covering one thread of the canvas. Bring the needle out
at 1, in at 2, out at 3, in at 4 , out at 5 and in at 6. This forms
one repeat. Work each one in the same way placing them next
to each other and coming into the same holes as the previous
repeat for a good coverage of the canvas.

Diagonal Stitches

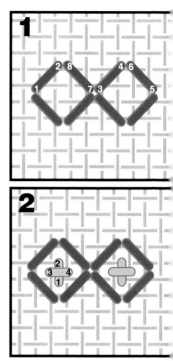

Working Instructions

Lattice Stitch is a very attractive diamond-shaped stitch usually worked in two colours. The diamonds can be worked individually to form small motifs on the canvas or details such as window panes. Alternatively, they can be worked together to form an all-over pattern which would be good for abstract designs or a flower garden especially if the centre crosses are stitched in different colours.

Work the diagonal lines first by bringing the needle out at 1 in at 2, out at 3, in at 4, out at 5, and so on. When you have worked the diamond shapes, fill the centre with an Upright Cross in a different colour. Bring the needle out at 1, in at 2, out at 3 and in at 4.

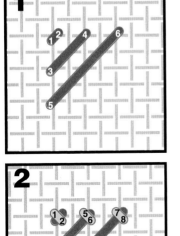

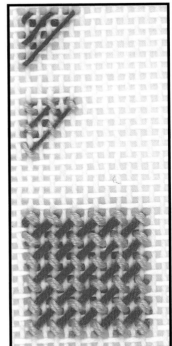

Working Instructions

Web Stitch is usually worked in two colours for effect but it can be worked in one if you prefer. It creates an interesting pattern on the canvas and is good for filling in background areas.

Work the diagonal stitches first across the canvas. Provided the tension is kept even while making these diagonal stitches you can work the small tying down stitches over them afterwards. This saves the bother of working with two needles. Work the diagonal stitches first, graduating their length across the canvas, then make the short diagonal stitches over them on alternate threads of the canvas. Stagger these stitches on each row to create a woven effect.

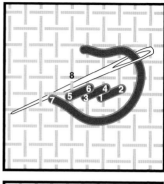

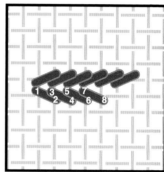

Working Instructions

Kelim Stitch is worked horizontally across the canvas to give a plaited effect. It is a dense stitch and is very good for covering the canvas. It can be used for filling large background areas and its density also lends it to small areas or motifs. Kelim Stitch, as its name suggests, is ideal for rugs.

Begin stitching from right to left. Bring the needle out at 1, in at 2, out at 3, in at 4, and so on. At the end of the row reverse the direction of the stitch by bringing the needle out at 1, in at 2 and continue stitching the next row in this way. Stitch the rows directly below each other coming out of the same holes as the previous row.

Straight Stitches

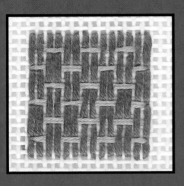

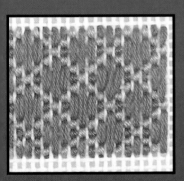
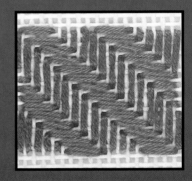

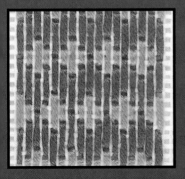
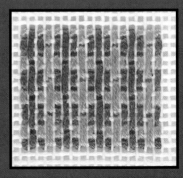

Straight Gobelin

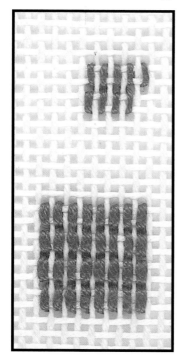

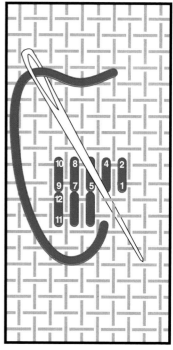

Working Instructions

Straight Gobelin is a very versatile stitch that covers the canvas well. It works equally well on small areas of the canvas as larger background areas. It can be worked to any length although it is best to avoid making the stitches too long or they will look loose and untidy. It is important to use wool or thread that is thick enough to cover the canvas beneath.

Work this stitch one row at a time. Bring the needle out at 1, in at 2, out at 3 and in at 4. Work the row beneath placing the stitches directly below the ones in the previous row.

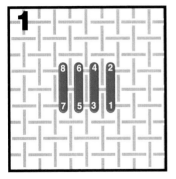

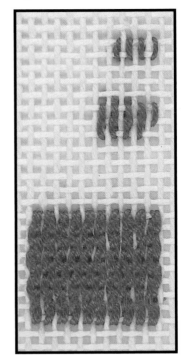

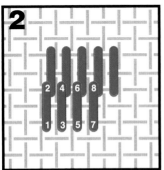

Working Instructions

Encroaching Straight Gobelin is similar to Straight Gobelin except that the rows overlap creating a denser appearance. This stitch can be used for small or large areas of the canvas and covers it better than Straight Gobelin. The stitches can be of any length but are usually no longer than five threads.

Work one row first from right to left then reverse the direction to work the next row below it from left to right. Place the tops of this row of stitches one thread above the base of the ones in the previous row and between two stitches to create an overlapping effect.

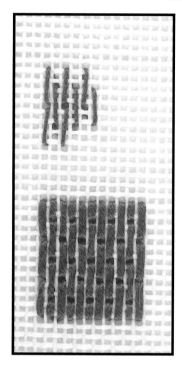

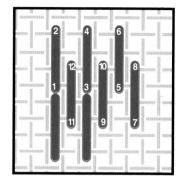

Working Instructions

Brick Stitch gives a textured appearance to the canvas and
the larger the area covered the better this effect will be. It can
be used as a general background stitch or, as the name
suggests, for brick patterns on houses. The stitches can cover
either two or four threads depending on the desired effect.

Work the top row first by bringing the needle out at 1, in at
2, out at 3, in at 4, and so on. The tops of the next row of
stitches should be positioned mid way between the stitches
of the previous row.

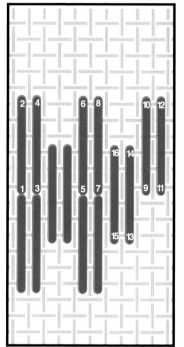 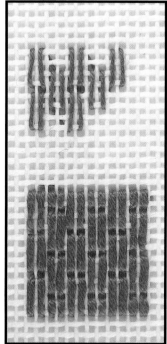

Working Instructions

Double Brick Stitch is formed in the same way as Brick Stitch except that the stitches are worked in pairs rather than singly. This gives a fuller, bolder effect than Brick Stitch which is ideal for roof tiles in pictorial work. It can also be used as a background stitch as it covers the canvas fairly quickly. It can either be worked in a single colour or in rows of different colours to give a shaded effect.

Bring the needle out at 1, in at 2, out at 3, in at 4, and so on. Leave a gap of two holes between each pair of stitches for the next row. Work this below the first one, positioning the tops of the stitches mid way between the ones in the previous row.

Straight Stitches

Straight Stitches

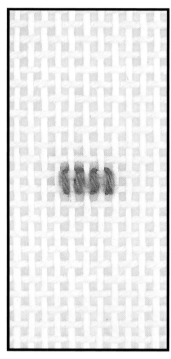

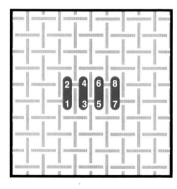

Working Instructions

Long Stitch gives a bolder more prominent outline than Backstitch. It can serve as a background filling stitch or outline details like flower stems or the edge of a house in pictorial work . Long Stitch can be worked to any length but care must be taken over tension to prevent the stitches sagging.

Bring the needle out at 1, in at 2, out at 3 and in at 4.

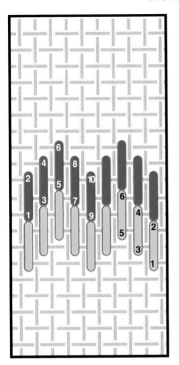

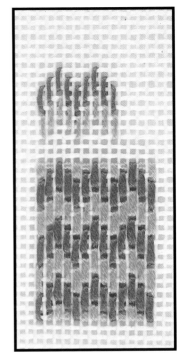

Working Instructions

Florentine Stitch is used in the type of work known as Florentine Embroidery but it is actually a needlepoint stitch. It is made up of straight stitches which step up and down to create a zig-zag pattern. In Basic Florentine Stitch these steps are evenly spaced as in the example shown here. However, in the many other variations these steps are unevenly spaced. Florentine Stitch can be worked in a single colour or in rows of different colours to create a more striking effect.

   Work the first row stepping the stitches up and down as you go. The second and subsequent rows are filled in exactly the same way: place the tops of the stitches in the new row in the same holes as the bottom of those in the previous one.

Straight Stitches

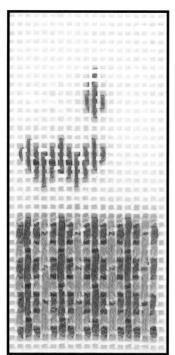

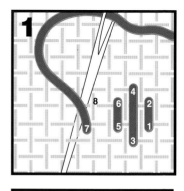

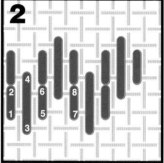

Working Instructions

Hungarian Stitch forms three-stitch diamonds across the canvas. After several rows a diagonal pattern of stitches is formed. This stitch is good for filling in background areas or for creating texture and interest in pictorial work.

Bring the needle out at 1, in at 2, out at 3, in at 4, out at 5 and in at 6 to form a repeat. Work a row in this way leaving a gap of one thread between each repeat. In the next row, position the longest stitch of each repeat in the gap between the repeats of the previous row. Follow the diagram for the exact placement of the stitches.

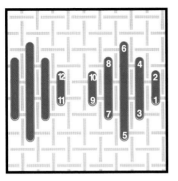

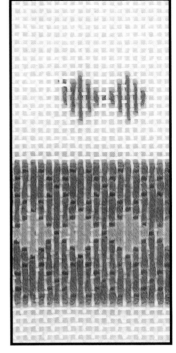

Working Instructions

Hungarian Diamond Stitch is made up of blocks of five straight stitches of graduating length. It is useful in pictorial work for giving a textured appearance to areas like floors, tablecloths or mats. Hungarian Diamond Stitch can be worked in a single colour as a background stitch or in different colours to create a striped or patterned effect.

Work one diamond at a time, bringing the needle out at 1, in at 2, out at 3, in at 4, and so on. Position the next diamond one thread to the left of the first diamond. When working rows position the diamonds beneath and between those in the first row. Work the rows from left to right and then from right to left.

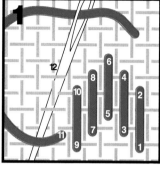

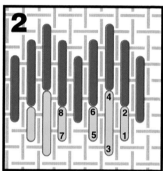

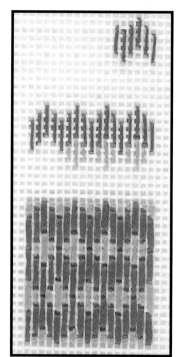

Working Instructions

Hungarian Grounding is made up of alternate rows of Hungarian Stitches and Florentine Stitches. This attractive stitch can be used for filling large background areas and is especially striking worked in two colours. For a more uniform appearance all the stitches can be worked in one colour.

Work a row of Florentine Stitches first, bringing the needle out at 1, in at 2, out at 3, in at 4, and so on, repeating the pattern of four straight stitches across the row. Make Hungarian Stitches beneath these, slotting them directly below the Florentine Stitches. Bring the needle out at 1, in at 2, out at 3, in at 4, out at 5 and in at 6. These three stitches form the basis of the next row. Continue in this way until you have filled the area.

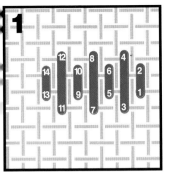

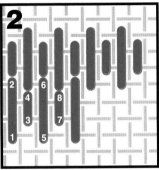

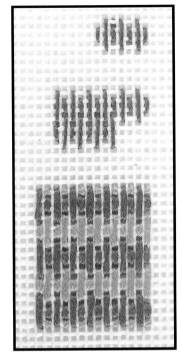

Working Instructions

Parisian Stitch is made up of two different length stitches which are repeated. It is a very easy pattern to work and produces an irregular texture which is useful for background stitching or for creating a varied effect on such areas as landscapes or fields. It can be worked in one colour for a uniform appearance or in two-colour stripes.

Bring the needle out at 1, in at 2, out at 3, in at 4, and so on. Repeat these two stitches to form a row. In further rows, slot the long stitches under the short ones in the previous row.

Diamond Straight

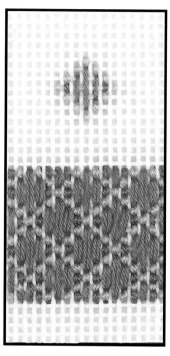

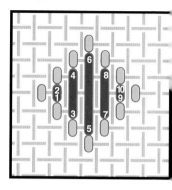

Working Instructions

Diamond Straight Stitch is a very attractive stitch which is best used over a large area. It can be used as an all-over stitch on a cushion cover or footstool. It consists of five straight stitches worked in a diamond shape with small stitches worked over one thread around each diamond. These small stitches are best made in a contrasting colour for full effect.

Work all the diamonds first by bringing the needle out at 1, in at 2, out at 3, in at 4, and so on, until you have worked all five stitches to form the diamond. Work the next diamond one thread away from the first one in the same way. When you have completed all the diamonds work the small straight stitches around them.

—— The Needlecraft Book of Needlepoint Stitches ——

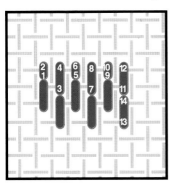

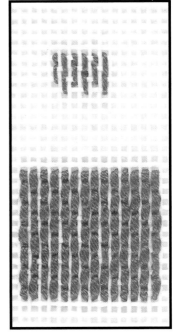

Working Instructions

Long and Short Stitch can be worked to any length but care must be taken over tension to keep the stitches even. It covers the canvas well and creates a brick-like effect which is useful for walls and roofs or for grassy areas. It can also be a background stitch, but does not cover the canvas very quickly unless the stitches are quite long. It is best worked in one colour to give a uniform appearance.

Work one row at a time, bringing the needle out at 1, in at 2, out at 3, in at 4, and so on. The stitches in the first row must be of different lengths for the positioning of the rows beneath. In the next row make all the stitches the same length as the long ones in the first row, stepping up and down each time. Make the last row of the block in the same way as the first.

—— The Needlecraft Book of Needlepoint Stitches ——

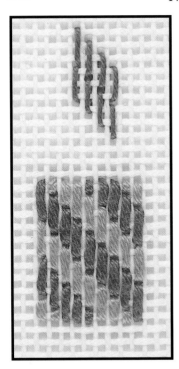

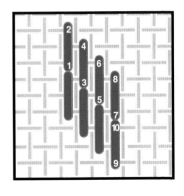

Working Instructions

Twill Stitch forms a stepped diagonal pattern which is very effective especially if worked in more than the one colour. It creates the effect of a diagonal stitch without distorting the canvas as much. It can be used in pictorial work for such areas as grass, fields and sky, as well as in patterned or abstract designs.

Work one diagonal row at a time in downward steps bringing the needle out at 1, in at 2, out at 3, and in at 4. Complete the row in this way; work the row beneath from the bottom upwards, making all the stitches the same length.

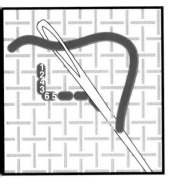

Working Instructions

Backstitch is one of the most versatile needlepoint stitches and is especially useful for pictorial work. It usually outlines detail or emphasises part of a picture. It can be used on detailed areas like window panes or stems which require only a thin line. Backstitch can be worked vertically, horizontally or diagonally. It is most commonly worked over one thread to give a solid bold line especially if it is in a darker shade than the area it is emphasising. Backstitch can be worked over any number of threads especially on an irregularly shaped outline. However, the stitches should not be too long.

Bring the needle out at 1, in at 2, along to 3 and back in at 4. Continue stitching the outline in this way, always working back on yourself.

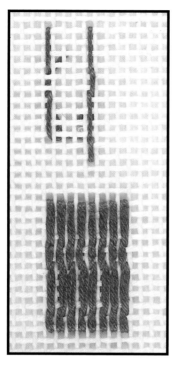

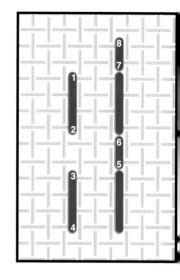

Working Instructions

Darning Stitch is a very closely worked stitch that covers the canvas well. It is fairly time consuming to work so is not ideal for large areas of the canvas. It is good for small areas requiring an interesting texture like fields or sky.

Darning Stitch is worked in two stages. In the first one, bring the needle out at 1, in at 2, under and out at 3, then in at 4. For the second stage bring the needle out at 5, in at 6, under the long stitch and out at 7, then in at 8 to produce a line of long and short stitches. Work all rows in the same way, making a line of long stitches first, and filling in the short stitches afterwards. The long and short stitches should always be directly beneath each other.

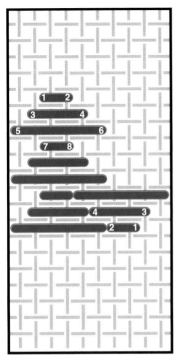

Working Instructions

Arrowhead Stitch is made up of three stitches of graduating length that form pyramids or arrowheads. As it is quite a large stitch it covers the canvas quickly. It is useful for large background areas as it does not distort the canvas and gives an attractive effect. It can be worked in only one colour or, for a wavy appearance, in lines of different colours. Lines of graduating shades of colour can be used for sky or sea.

Work one vertical row at a time, bringing the needle out at 1, in at 2, out at 3, in at 4, out at 5 and in at 6 to form one Arrowhead. Work the next Arrowhead directly below placing the top stitch beneath the long stitch of the previous one. On the next row reverse the direction of the Arrowheads so that the short stitches lie next to the long ones of the previous row.

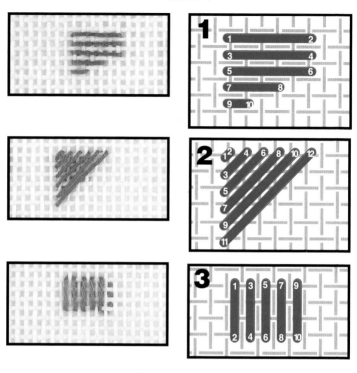

Working Instructions

Satin Stitch can be worked in any direction and to any length. It forms the basis of many other needlepoint stitches and is therefore one of the most important stitches to learn. It covers the canvas well and can be worked to any shape required.

Satin Stitch gives a raised appearance as it has the same number of stitches on the back as on the front so it is useful in pictorial work for areas which need to be prominent.

Bring the needle out at 1, in at 2, under and out at 3, across to 4, and so on. Always work in this "over and under" way to give the stitch its raised appearance. Graduate the length of the stitches to fill the area required.

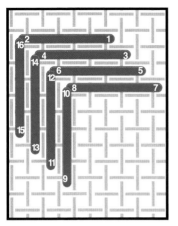

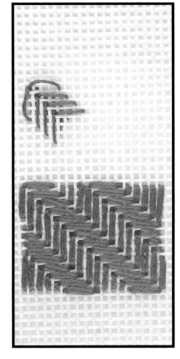

Working Instructions

Chevron Stitch is made up of a combination of horizontal and vertical straight stitches. It can be worked in only one colour, as the light falls differently on the vertical and horizontal stitches giving the appearance of different shades. However, for a more dramatic effect, work the stitch in different colours. Chevron Stitch can be useful in pictorial work for giving the appearance of dimension, such as on a sloping roof.

Work the horizontal stitches in one diagonal row first, bringing the needle out at 1, in at 2, out at 3, in at 4, and so on, moving the stitches one thread to the right each time but keeping them the same length. Next, work the vertical stitches, coming into the same holes as the stitches in the first row and moving up one thread at a time as shown.

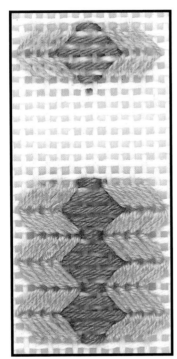

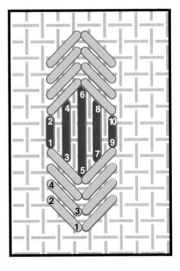

Working Instructions

Indian Stripe can be stitched on its own or in groups either horizontally or vertically. It looks most effective as part of a border design, especially if worked in two colours. The centre of Indian Stripe is a Hungarian Diamond and the outer parts are diagonal stitches.

Work the central diamond first bringing the needle out at 1, in at 2, out at 3, in at 4, and so on until you have completed the five stitches forming the diamond. Next, work the diagonal stitches on either side of the diamond. When making rows of Indian Stripes, the bottom short stitch of the first diamond becomes the top short stitch of the second stripe as shown. Remember to work all the diamonds first and the diagonal outer stitches afterwards, especially if using different colours.

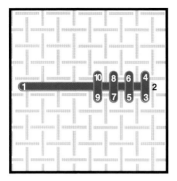

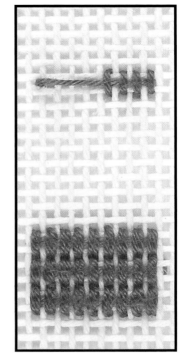

Working Instructions

Tramming is a method of giving a raised appearance to stitching without the tramming threads being visible afterwards. It is ideal for making needlepoint more hard wearing especially on footstools and kneelers. Continental Tent Stitch, Cross Stitch and Straight Gobelin can all be worked over a tramming thread.

Bring the needle out at 1 then carry the thread across the canvas to where you want your finished line to be, and push it back in at 2. Bring the needle out at 3 and stitch back over the tramming thread. The example shows Straight Gobelin being worked over a tramming thread.

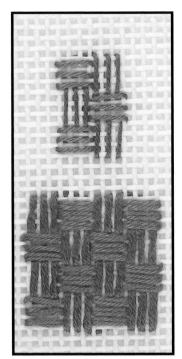

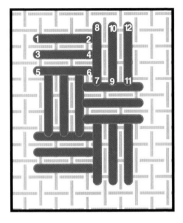

Working Instructions

Weaving Stitch gives the appearance of threads that have been woven together. This stitch is much easier to work than it appears and is formed of groups of three straight stitches worked horizontally and vertically next to each other. It can be used as a background stitch in patterned work or for pictorial details like baskets or floors. Weaving stitch can be worked in a single colour to give a basketwork effect or in two colours for a chequerboard appearance.

Begin by working three horizontal stitches, bringing the needle out at 1, in at 2, out at 3, in at 4, out at 5 and in at 6. Next, work three horizontal stitches against the vertical ones. Take care not to split the threads of the last vertical stitches.

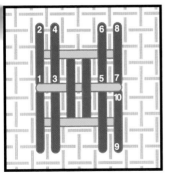

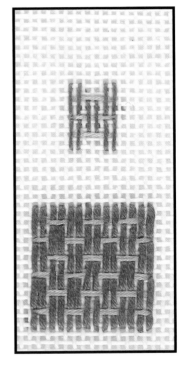

Working Instructions

Willow Stitch is worked in the same way as Double Brick Stitch except for the extra thread that is woven through it. It is good for backgrounds but can also be used in pictorial work for roof tiles or baskets. It is best worked in two colours with the weaving stitch in a contrasting colour to the vertical stitches.

Work all the vertical stitches first, bringing the needle out at 1, in at 2, out at 3, in at 4, and so on. Work the next row of stitches centrally between the first row as shown. When you have completed all the vertical stitches, take a different thread and weave it under the first block, over the join between the two rows, under the next block and so on, always keeping the thread running in a straight line.

Straight Stitches

Crossing Stitches

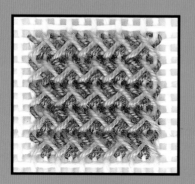

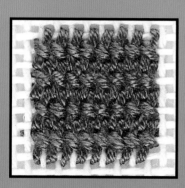
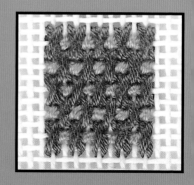
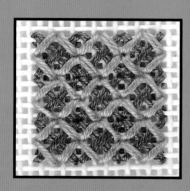

Cross Stitch

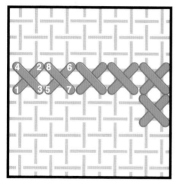

Working Instructions

Cross Stitch is a small stitch which is good for background areas or landscapes requiring a varied texture. It is made up of two diagonal stitches worked in opposite directions to cross over each other. It usually only crosses over one canvas thread. Cross Stitch can be worked vertically, horizontally or diagonally depending on the area to be filled. The tops of the crosses should always face in the same direction.

Bring the needle out at 1, in at 2, out at 3 and in at 4 to complete the cross. Work the next crosses beside each other, and further rows with the crosses directly below each other. Another method of working Cross Stitch is to make a row of all the stitches in one direction first, then work back along the row reversing the direction of these stitches to form crosses.

—— The Needlecraft Book of Needlepoint Stitches ——

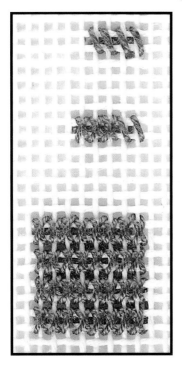

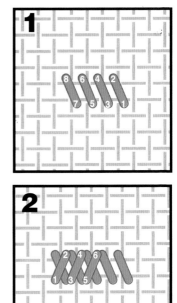

Working Instructions

Oblong Cross Stitch is formed in the same way as Cross Stitch but is elongated to form a rectangular rather than a square stitch. It does not provide such a dense coverage of the canvas as Cross Stitch giving a slightly different texture that is suitable for filling background areas.

Work the stitches facing in one direction first by bringing the needle out at 1, in at 2, out at 3 and in at 4. When you have made these stitches work back along the row, reversing the direction of the stitches to cross over the ones already worked. Work the next row of Oblong Cross Stitches directly beneath the first row.

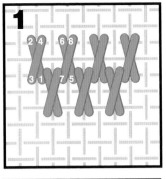

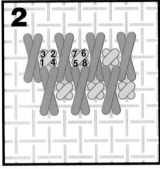

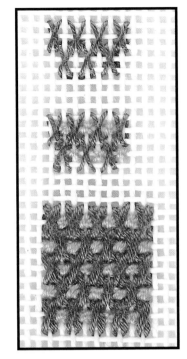

Working Instructions

Double Stitch is made up of a combination of Oblong Cross Stitch and Cross Stitch. It can all be worked in one colour as a background stitch or in two colours for a more attractive patterned effect. The stitch consists of rows of Oblong Cross Stitches with Cross Stitches worked between them. The larger crosses are three threads in height.

Work a row of Oblong Crosses first by bringing the needle out at 1, in at 2, out at 3 and in at 4. Leave a gap of one thread between each cross. In the next row position the stitches between those in the first row, placing the tops of the crosses one thread above the bottom of the stitches in the previous row. Fill in the remaining gaps with Cross Stitches.

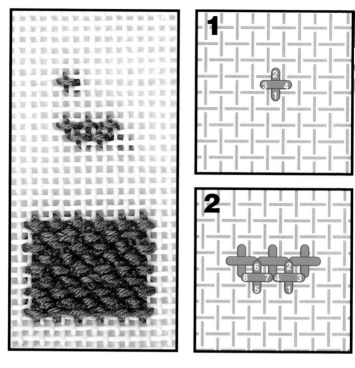

Working Instructions

Upright Cross Stitch gives good coverage and an interesting texture. It can be used in background areas, landscapes or any patterned work. The stitch covers two threads of the canvas and consists of two straight stitches, one horizontal and one vertical, that cross in the centre.

Work one stitch at a time bringing the needle out at 1, in at 2, out at 3 and in at 4. Work all the stitches in one row beside each other so that the horizontal threads form a straight line. In the next row position the Upright Cross Stitches one thread to the right of those in the previous row to avoid any gaps.

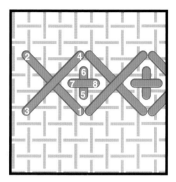

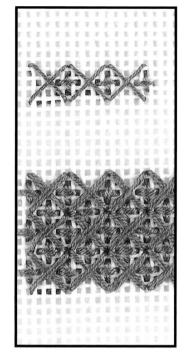

Working Instructions

Double Cross Stitch creates a lattice work effect which is very good for patterned work. It is made up of large Cross Stitches which cover four threads with Upright Cross Stitches in between. For a more attractive effect, work the Upright Cross Stitches in a different colour to the Cross Stitches.

Begin by working a large cross, bringing the needle out at 1, in at 2, out at 3 and in at 4. Next, work an Upright Cross to the right of this, bringing the needle out at 5, in at 6, out at 7 and in at 8. Complete the row in this way making sure that the points of the large crosses touch. Work the next row in the same way directly below the first one. When you have covered the area, go back and fill in the gaps between the large cross stitches with Upright Crosses as shown.

The Needlecraft Book of Needlepoint Stitches

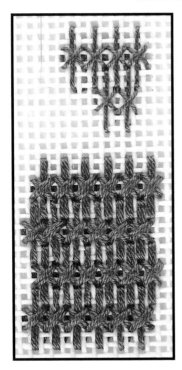

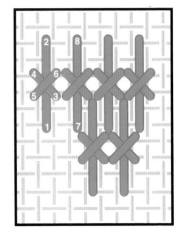

Working Instructions

Crossed Gobelin is fairly quick to work and covers the canvas quite well. It is good for patterned designs or as an abstract background stitch. It consists of a straight stitch worked over six threads of the canvas with a Cross Stitch over the top.

Begin by working the straight stitch bringing the needle out at 1 and in at 2. Next, work the Cross Stitch centrally over this bringing the needle out at 3, in at 4, out at 5 and in at 6. Work the next vertical stitch two threads away from the first one on the same level. The points of the crosses should touch in each row. In the next row place the tops of the straight stitches in the hole where the points of the Crosses in the first row meet.

Crossing Stitches

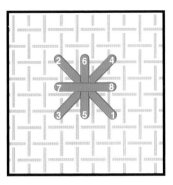

Working Instructions

Leviathan Stitch is also known as Smyrna Stitch. This stitch can be used either as a single motif in pictorial work or to form patterns. It is made up of four stitches which all cross in the centre. Take care to work each stitch in the correct order or your work will look untidy.

To work a Leviathan Stitch bring the needle out at 1, across and in at 2, down and out at 3, across to 4, out at 5, in at 6, out at 7 and finally, in at 8. Place further Leviathan Stitches side by side and directly below each other.

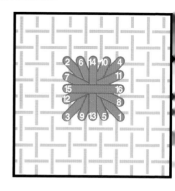

Working Instructions

Double Leviathan Stitch gives a more dense coverage of the canvas than Leviathan Stitch. Again, it can be used as a single motif or in blocks to create a patterned effect. Both variations are the same size but on the double version eight stitches cross at the centre. Follow the diagram carefully to ensure that you work the stitches in the correct order.

Bring the needle out at 1, in at 2, out at 3, in at 4, and so on, following the numbers on the diagram. Further Double Leviathan Stitches should be placed directly beside and beneath each other as shown.

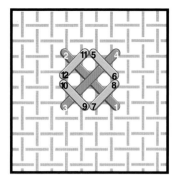

Working Instructions

Rice Stitch is a very attractive stitch which covers the canvas well. It can be a single motif but is best worked in blocks to form patterns. It is usually stitched in two colours with the large Cross Stitch in one colour and the small diagonal stitches over each corner in a contrasting colour.

Begin by stitching the large cross bringing the needle out at 1, in at 2, out at 3 and in at 4. Next, work a small diagonal stitch over each corner making their points touch. Position further Rice Stitches with the large crosses directly beside each other and in further rows directly beneath each other. It is easier to work all the large crosses first and the diagonal stitches over them afterwards.

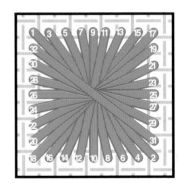

Working Instructions

Rhodes Stitch gives a very dense, three-dimensional effect as all the threads cross at the centre making the stitch raised. It usually forms a single motif but can make an effective border. Rhodes Stitch covers a square area of the canvas of any size. Great care must be taken over tension to prevent the stitches either sagging or, if too tight, distorting the canvas.

Follow the numbers on the diagram carefully and work the stitches in the correct order. Bring the needle out at the top left-hand corner of the square at 1 and across to the bottom right-hand corner at 2, bring the needle back out at 3 then over to 4, and so on. Further Rhodes Stitches should be positioned directly beside or beneath each other.

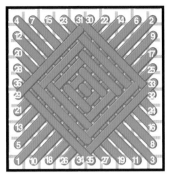

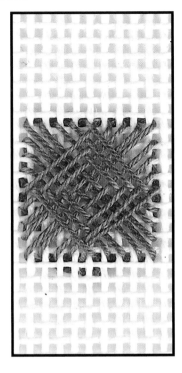

Working Instructions

Norwich Stitch is another three-dimensional stitch which looks attractive as a single motif. It can also be worked as repeats in patterned work or in rows as a border. It looks complicated but if you follow the numbers carefully, is fairly easy to work.

Bring the needle out at the bottom left-hand corner at 1, and move across to the top right-hand corner at 2. Take the needle down to 3, and over to 4 at the opposite corner, and so on. On the final stitch from 35 to 36, thread the needle under the 29–30 stitch and into the canvas at 36 to complete.

 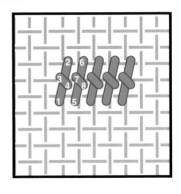

Working Instructions

Knotted Stitch consists of long diagonal stitches secured by a short diagonal stitch worked over the centre. This stitch produces a dense coverage of the canvas and is useful for filling background areas or for creating a textured, striped appearance in pictorial work.

Bring the needle out at 1 and up in to 2, take the needle out at 3 then back over to 4. This forms one knotted stitch. Place further stitches in the row beside each other following the numbers on the diagram. In the next row position the tops of the long diagonal stitches between two stitches of the previous row and one thread up from where they end.

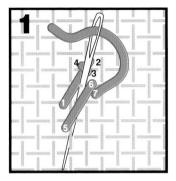

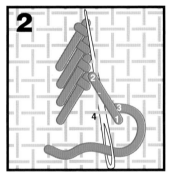

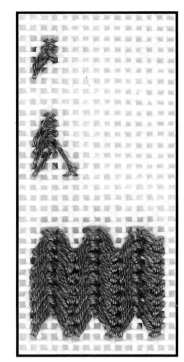

Working Instructions

Fishbone Stitch, as its name suggests, produces an interlocking pattern rather like a fishbone. It forms stripes which give a wavelike effect to the canvas. Fishbone Stitch is a dense stitch which gives good coverage of the canvas and can be used as a background stitch. It can also form a motif like tall flowers with Backstitch added for the stems.

Begin at the top of the stitch and work downwards in rows bringing the needle out at 1, in at 2, out at 3, in at 4, out at 5 and in at 6. To work the other side of the stitch, reverse the direction in which you work bringing the needle out at 1, in at 2, out at 3, in at 4, and so on. Subsequent repeats should be placed beside each other and on the same level.

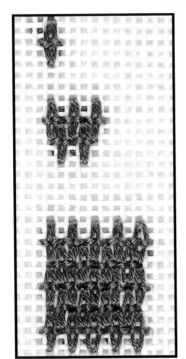

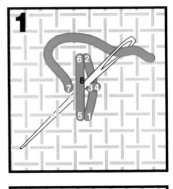

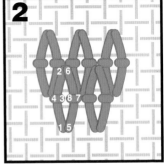

Working Instructions

French Stitch is made up of two straight vertical stitches held apart by two small horizontal stitches. It gives quite a good coverage of the canvas so can be used as a background stitch. Single French Stitches are seldom used as they are much more effective worked in repeats for patterned work.

Bring the needle out at 1 and in at 2 to form the first straight stitch – do not pull it too tightly or this will spoil the curved appearance. Bring the needle out again at 3, over the first stitch at 4, out at the bottom at 5, then up and in at 6. Work the last stitch over this by coming out at 7 and in at the centre at 8. Position the French Stitches in subsequent rows with the tops of the vertical stitches in the same holes as the horizontal stitches in the row above.

Working Instructions

Rococo Stitch is formed in a similar way to French Stitch but is larger and more attractive. It can be used as a small motif in patterned work or as repeats for a background stitch but is not often used in pictorial work.

Bring the needle out at 1 and in at 2, but do not pull tightly or it will not curve easily when you work a short stitch across it bringing the needle out at 3 and in at 4. Work another vertical stitch, bringing the needle out at 5 and in at 6, then a small stitch across it, bringing the needle out at 7 and in at 8. Refer to the diagram to work the other half of the stitch. Place Rococo Stitches beside each other to form a row. Further rows should be positioned between the stitches in the row above.

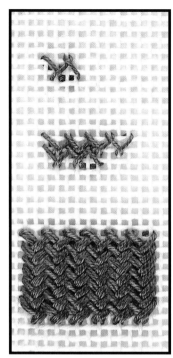

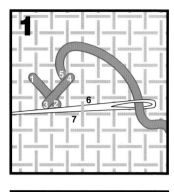

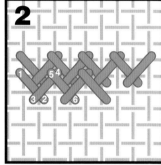

Working Instructions

Herringbone Stitch is a dense and hard-wearing stitch which is ideal for footstools or rugs. When worked over large areas an attractive texture is achieved. This stitch is worked in rows across the canvas.

Begin by bringing the needle out at 1, in at 2, across to 3, then over to 4, crossing over the first stitch. Bring the needle out again at 5 and in at 6 as in the first stitch. Complete the row in this way. Weave the thread through the back of the stitches you have just worked, then work further rows one thread directly below the first one in the same way.

Double Herringbone

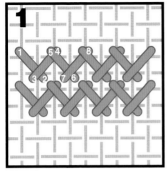

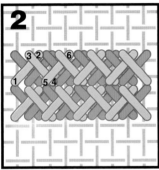

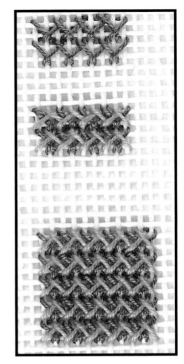

Working Instructions

Double Herringbone Stitch is formed in the same way as Herringbone Stitch except that rows of stitches facing the opposite direction are worked on top of the first layer of stitches. It is even more hard-wearing stitch than Herringbone Stitch and is ideal for rugmaking or footstools. It is usually worked in two colours to produce an attractive pattern.

Work Herringbone Stitch first across the whole area as in the first diagram. Weave the thread through the back of the stitches to begin again from the left two threads below the first stitch of the previous row. When you have filled the area, go over these stitches again in the same way but this time stitch them upside down. Bring the needle out at 1, in at 2, out at 3, in at 4, and so on. Again, space the rows two threads apart.

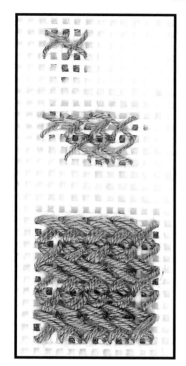

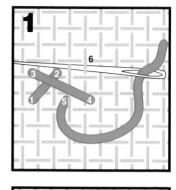

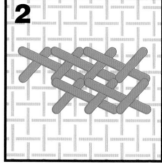

Working Instructions

Greek Stitch produces a plaited effect and is quite a dense stitch that can be used to fill background areas. It creates an attractive texture which can be useful in pictorial work.

Each row is worked from left to right. Bring the needle out at 1, across and in at 2, under to 3 and across to 4. Take the needle back out at 5 and over to 6. At the end of the row turn the canvas upside down and work the next row directly below.

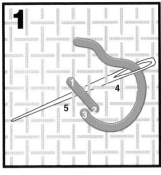

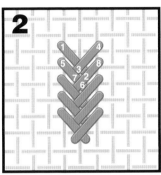

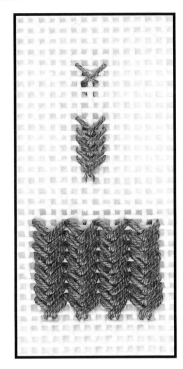

Working Instructions

Fern Stitch produces a striped effect that covers the canvas well. It is useful for filling background areas but is most effective where definite patterned areas are required such as in fields or landscapes.

Begin at the top left-hand corner of the area bringing the needle out at 1, over and in at 2, across and out at 3, then over the first stitch into 4. Work the next stitch in the same way one thread below and over the first stitch. Take the thread up behind the first row to work the next one beginning at the right-hand edge of the previous row.

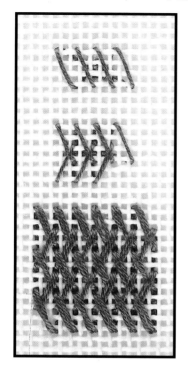

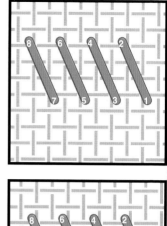

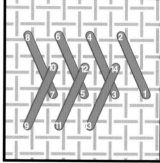

Working Instructions

Plaited Stitch gives a woven appearance and is mostly used in patterned work. As the stitches are fairly long choose a thread that will be thick enough to cover the canvas. It can be stitched in just one colour or in rows of alternating colours for a more varied effect.

Begin by bringing the needle out at 1, across and in at 2, down and out at 3, then in at 4. Work a row of diagonal stitches in this way then work the next row from left to right reversing the direction of the stitches and crossing over those in the first row. Bring the needle out at 9, across and in at 10, back down and out at 11, in at 12, and so on.

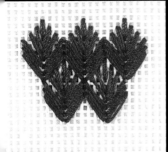

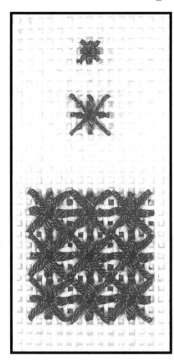

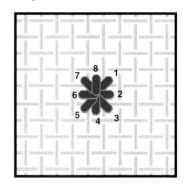

Working Instructions

Algerian Eye Stitch is made up of eight stitches worked in a star-like formation. It can be stitched over one or two threads, as shown in the diagram, but is always worked in the same way. Algerian Eye Stitch is useful for small motifs like stars. Blocks of small or large Algerian Eye Stitches can be used to cover areas of the canvas. Use a thread which is thick enough to cover the canvas underneath, but will not distort the centre hole which is stitched into eight times.

Begin from the top right and work into the centre each time. Bring the needle out at 1, into the centre, out at 2, into the centre, out at 3, and so on. If the canvas shows through between the Algerian Eyes, work backstitches around each one to cover this.

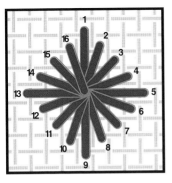

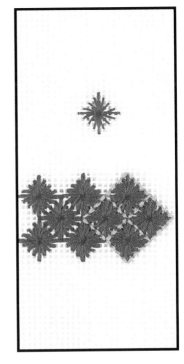

Working Instructions

Diamond Eyelet Stitch is a large and attractive stitch made up of 16 stitches. It is can be used singly for small motifs or worked in blocks to cover the canvas. You may need to work backstitches in either the same or a different colour between each Eyelet to prevent the canvas showing through. Use thread which is thick enough to cover the canvas but will not distort the central hole.

Bring the needle out at the centre, across four threads and in at 1, out at the centre, in at 2, and so on until you have worked back round to where you started. Work a row of Diamond Eyelets beside each other. In following rows slot each Eyelet between the ones in the row above.

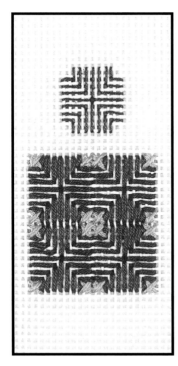

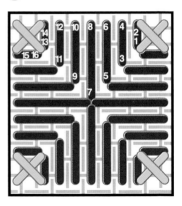

Working Instructions

Triangle Stitch is a large motif which can be used alone or to form a very attractive and uniform pattern which is good as a background stitch or for abstract designs. It is made up of four triangles which join in the centre with Cross Stitches at each corner to fill in the gaps. It can be worked all in one colour or with the Cross Stitches in a different colour to the triangles.

Work one triangle at a time, bringing the needle out at 1, in at 2, out at 3, in at 4, and so on. When you have stitched the triangles, work the Cross Stitches in each corner. When covering an area with Triangle Stitches you can stitch all the Cross Stitches after you have completed all the triangles, especially if you are using a different colour for these.

Composite Stitches

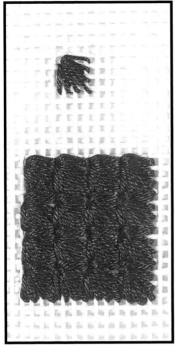 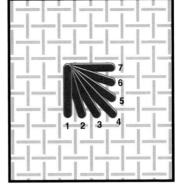

Working Instructions

Ray Stitch covers the canvas well. It can either be used for single motifs like small trees or bushes, or it can be worked as a background stitch. Ray Stitch can be stitched in one colour or, for a more effective appearance, in two-colour stripes.

Ray Stitch is made up of seven stitches with each one worked from the same point in the top left-hand corner. Bring the needle out at this point, in at 1, out at the top, in at 2, and so on to complete a Ray. Work subsequent Rays in the same way positioning the vertical stitch at the beginning of the next one across the last four stitches of the previous one.

Composite Stitches

Working Instructions

Fan Stitch is a fairly open stitch which can be used alone in pictorial work for stars, bushes, trees or abstract motifs. It can also be used to cover an area of background. Each Fan consists of five stitches which all radiate from the same point. To create a striped or patterned effect, work each row in a different colour. It is advisable to use a thread which adequately covers the canvas.

Bring the needle out in the bottom left-hand corner at A, in at 1, out at A, in at 2, and so on until you have completed five stitches. Work the Fans in rows positioning them next to and directly below each other as shown.

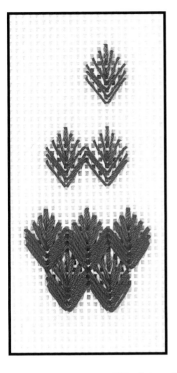

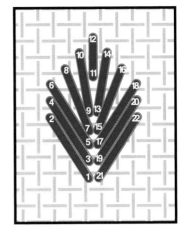

Working Instructions

Leaf Stitch is a large stitch which can be used singly in pictorial work for motifs like leaves and trees or as a background stitch. For further detail you could add backstitches through the centre of the Leaf to make a stem. Choose a thread which will cover the canvas underneath.

Bring the needle out at the centre bottom at 1, in at 2, out at 3, in at 4, and so on to form a Leaf. To make a larger Leaf, add more stitches to the sides, and keep the top five stitches the same. Work one row of Leaf Stitches at a time positioning each Leaf next to the last one. In subsequent rows slot each Leaf beneath the ones in the previous row as shown.

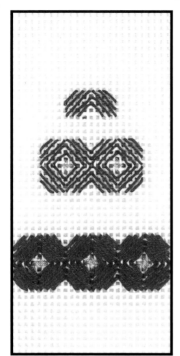

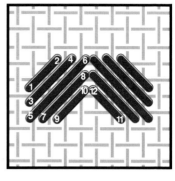

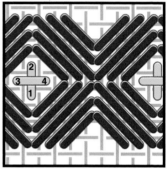

Working Instructions

Brighton Stitch should be worked in rows to achieve the best effect. It gives a good coverage of the canvas and is a hard-wearing stitch that is ideal for footstools. It is made up of blocks of graduating diagonal stitches with Upright Cross Stitches worked in the centre to fill the gaps. Brighton Stitch can all be worked in the one colour but it looks more effective if the crosses are in a contrasting colour.

Work one row at a time, bringing the needle out at 1, in at 2, out at 3, in at 4, and so on. Position the next diagonal block to the right of the first but reverse the direction of the stitches. Follow the diagram for the position of subsequent blocks reversing the direction of the stitches each time. Work upright Cross Stitches in the centre of each one as shown.

—— The Needlecraft Book of Needlepoint Stitches ——

Knotted Stitches

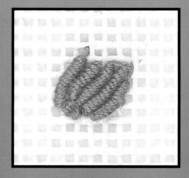

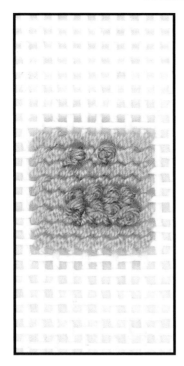

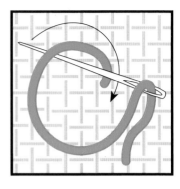

Working Instructions

French Knots are useful for any small detail on a piece of work. They are usually positioned over other canvas stitches and can be worked singly or in groups. Stitched closely together they can fill an area like bushes and trees. It is important to keep the knots even. Work them in the way shown and you should always achieve neat tight knots.

Holding the thread with your left hand, twist the needle round the thread twice (do not twist the thread round the needle). Insert the point of the needle back into the canvas and pull up the thread in order to tighten the knot. Push the needle back into the canvas close to where the thread emerges. The size of the knot is determined by the number of times that you twist the needle round the thread.

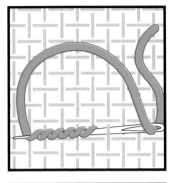

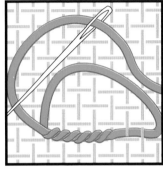

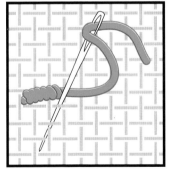

Working Instructions

Bullion Knots provide useful detail on pictorial work. Bring the needle out and push it in further over. Bring it out where the thread emerges to set the length of the stitch. Do not pull the needle all the way through. Wrap the thread around the needle as many times as the length requires. Hold the twists with your thumb and pull the needle through the canvas and the twists. Pull the needle and twists back the other way to make the coil lie flat. Push the needle back in and over to where the stitch began.

—— The Needlecraft Book of Needlepoint Stitches ——

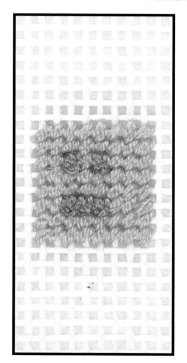

Knotted Stitches

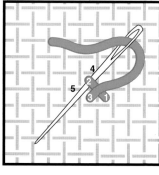

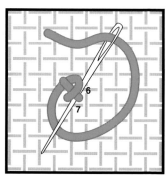

Working Instructions

Danish Knots can be used singly for small details like eyes or clustered together in groups to fill an area of the canvas.

Bring the needle out at 1 and across and in at 2 to form a diagonal stitch. Bring the needle out at 3, then thread it under the diagonal stitch at 4, and out the other side at 5. Take the needle back under the other side of

the stitch at 6, and out at 7. To finish, take the thread over to 8 and through to the back of the canvas.

Index of Stitches

Index